TREASURY OF LITEF

Language Handbook
Grade 1

Copyright © by Harcourt Brace & Company

All rights reserved. No part of this publication may be reproduced or transmitted in
any form or by any means, electronic or mechanical, including photocopy, recording,
or any information storage and retrieval system.

Requests for permission to make copies of any part of the work should be mailed to:
Permissions Department, Harcourt Brace & Company, 6277 Sea Harbor Drive,
Orlando, Florida 32887-6777.

Printed in the United States of America

ISBN 0-15-303581-1

4 5 6 7 8 9 10   073   97 96 95

THIS BOOK IS PRINTED ON **ACID-FREE, RECYCLED PAPER.**

HARCOURT BRACE & COMPANY
ORLANDO · ATLANTA · AUSTIN · BOSTON · SAN FRANCISCO · CHICAGO · DALLAS · NEW YORK
TORONTO · LONDON

Contents

LETTER TO THE STUDENT viii

WRITING

The Writing Process 2
Sentences About a Picture 3
Story About You 4
Poem 5
Friendly Letter 6
Description 7
Story 8
Riddle 9
Book Report 10
How-to Sentences 11
Scene 12

GRAMMAR, USAGE, AND MECHANICS

Sentences 14
- Word Order in Sentences 15
- Telling Sentences 16
- Asking Sentences 17
- Naming Parts of Sentences 18
- Joining Naming Parts 19
- Telling Parts of Sentences 20
- Joining Telling Parts 21
- Is It a Sentence? 22
- Writing I 23
- End Marks 24
  - KIDS ON LANGUAGE 25

Naming Words 26
- Naming Words for People 27
- Naming Words for Places 28
- Naming Words for Animals and Things 29
- Special Names and Titles of People 30
- Names of Special Places 31
- One and More Than One 32
- Days of the Week 33
- Months 34
- Holidays 35

Using I and Me 36

Using He, She, and It 37
    KIDS ON LANGUAGE......................38

Describing Words 39
    Feelings 40
    Size and Shape 41
    Taste and Smell.......................42
    Colors and Numbers...................43
    Feel and Sound 44
    Describing Words with er
       and est 45
    Describing Words for Weather 46
    KIDS ON LANGUAGE......................47

Action Words 48
    Action Words About the Past 49
    Action Words About Now 50
    Is and Are 51
    Go and Went 52
    Was and Were 53
    KIDS ON LANGUAGE......................54

HANDWRITING

Uppercase Manuscript Alphabet.....56
Lowercase Manuscript Alphabet.....57
Elements of Handwriting 58
Common Errors—l, h, n 60
Common Errors—c, d, o 61
Common Errors—f, a, k, x 62
Common Errors—T, E, Q...............63
Common Errors—G, U, R 64
Common Errors—D, M, W, Z........65

WRITING FRAMES

Sentences About a Picture 66
Story 67
Poem 68
Friendly Letter................................69
Book Report 70

INDEX 71

Dear Student,

The <u>Language Handbook</u> will help you speak and write better. It will help you choose the right words to tell about something. Inside are many ideas for writing, too. We hope you have fun learning about your language.

Sincerely,

The Authors

THE WRITING PROCESS

A story or a poem is easy to write when you have a plan. First, think about <u>what</u> you want to write, <u>who</u> you are writing for, and <u>why</u> you are writing. Then, use these five stages to plan your writing.

PREWRITING
Make a list of ideas to write about. Draw a picture or make a chart of the idea you choose.

DRAFTING
Write about your prewriting idea.
Do not worry about making a mistake.

RESPONDING AND REVISING
Meet with a partner to talk about your draft.

PROOFREADING
Reread or read aloud your revised draft.

PUBLISHING
Think about how you want to share your work.

Name _____

Sentences About a Picture

When you draw a picture, you can write about it. Answer the questions **Who? What? Where?** and **When?**

1. Draw your picture.
2. Think about what you want to write.
3. Answer the questions Who? What? Where? and When?

MODEL: SENTENCES ABOUT A PICTURE

Jack is my dog. I walk him after school. Sometimes he chases Hooper. Hooper is a cat.

WRITING

Teacher/Family Member: Read and discuss the page with children. Help them refer to the information when they write sentences about a picture.

Name _____

Story About You

A **story about you** is one kind of story you can write. In a story about you, you tell about something that you did.

1. **Think about things you have done. Choose one to write about.**
2. **Write your story. Tell in order what you did.**
3. **Use words like <u>I</u> and <u>me</u>.**

MODEL: STORY ABOUT YOU

First, I learned to sing "Twinkle, Twinkle, Little Star." Next, I learned to play it on the piano. Now, you can sing with me while I play it!

WRITING

Teacher/Family Member: Read and discuss the page with children. Help them refer to the information when they write a personal narrative.

Name _____

Poem

You can write a **poem.** Some poems have rhyming words. Rhyming words are words that end with the same sound.

1. **Choose something to write about.**
2. **Think of rhyming words or other words to use.**
3. **Write your poem.**

MODEL: POEM

The <u>snake</u> ate the <u>cake</u>.
The <u>bear</u> ate the <u>pear</u>.
The <u>bees</u> ate the <u>cheese</u>
But <u>I</u> ate the <u>pie</u>!

WRITING

Name _____

Friendly Letter

You can write a **friendly letter** to someone you know. In it, you tell something about yourself. A friendly letter has five parts.

1. **Think about things to tell about yourself. Choose one idea.**
2. **Write a letter to your friend.**
3. **Use the five parts that are shown by the arrows.**

MODEL: FRIENDLY LETTER

July 29, 1994

Dear Henry,

   I like my new home. At first, I didn't know who would be my friend. Then I met Jake. We played ball. Now he is my friend, and so are you!

   Your friend,
   Danny

WRITING

Teacher/Family Member: Read and discuss the page with children. Help them refer to the information when they write a friendly letter.

Name _____

Description

When you write a **description**, you tell about something. You use words that tell how the thing looks, sounds, tastes, smells, or feels.

1. Think about things you have seen. Choose one to write about.
2. Write a description. Tell what the thing was like.
3. Use detail words to tell how it looked, sounded, tasted, smelled, or felt.

MODEL: DESCRIPTION

The Fish Store

Our class went to a fish store. It was small and dark inside. There were many pretty fish. We watched a girl feed the fish. Then they swam fast!

Name _____

Story

You can write a **story** about someone or something. Tell who your story is about and what happens.

1. **Think of ideas for a story. Choose one to write about.**
2. **Write your story. Tell who it is about and what happens.**
3. **Write a title for your story.**

MODEL: STORY

Getting Together

Cat had a new ball. Pig had a new bat. They both wanted to play baseball. Cat and Pig got together. Then they had fun playing ball.

8

WRITING

Teacher/Family Member: Read and discuss the page with children. Help them refer to the information when they write a story.

Name _____

Riddle

A **riddle** is a word puzzle. You write clues in a riddle. Your friends guess what the riddle is about!

1. Think of things you can write riddles about. Choose one.
2. Write your clues. Ask a question at the end.
3. Turn your paper around and write the answer.

MODEL: RIDDLE

I am a fruit.
I am long and yellow.
I am white inside.
Monkeys like to eat me.
What am I?

(a banana)

WRITING

Teacher/Family Member: Read and discuss the page with children. Help them refer to the information when they write a riddle.

Name _____

Book Report

You can write a **book report** that tells about a book you have read.

1. Write the name of the book. Underline it.
2. Write the author's name.
3. Tell who or what the book is about. Tell your favorite part.

MODEL: BOOK REPORT

<u>Birthday Cookies</u>
by Ann Wilson

The book is about Tom. He and his mother bake lots of cookies. Tom takes them to school for his birthday. My favorite part is when the other children eat all the cookies.

Name _____

How-to Sentences

How-to sentences tell how to do or make something. When you write about how to do something, tell the steps in order.

1. **Think about things you know how to do. Choose one to write about.**
2. **Write how to do that thing. Tell the steps in the right order.**
3. **Use words like <u>first</u> and <u>last</u>.**

MODEL: HOW-TO SENTENCES

I can play hide-and-seek. You can, too. You need places to hide and some friends to play with. First, close your eyes. Then, count to ten while your friends hide. Last, go and find your friends!

WRITING

Teacher/Family Member: Read and discuss the page with children. Help them refer to the information when they write how-to sentences.

Scene

A **scene** is one kind of story. When you write a scene, you tell who is speaking. Then you write the words that character says.

1. **Think about characters. Choose some to write about.**
2. **Think about what happens to the characters.**
3. **Write the scene. Use the exact words the characters say.**

MODEL: SCENE

Lion: I can't find Mouse!
Rabbit: I will help you look.
Lion: Mouse, where are you?
Mouse: Here I am, Lion.
Rabbit: He's in your mane!
Lion: Mouse was here all the time!

Name _____

SENTENCES

A **sentence** is a group of words. It tells a complete idea. A sentence begins with a capital letter.

I see two eyes.

Two of these groups of words are sentences. Write the two sentences.

1. I see one nose.

2. will a happy face

3. You see my cap.

4. brown fox

Name _____

WORD ORDER IN SENTENCES

Words in a sentence are in order. The words must be in order to make sense.

Leo runs fast.

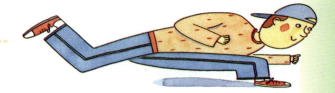

Write each sentence correctly.

1. can I run.

2. play. You can

3. happy. am I

4. I nap. will

Name _____

TELLING SENTENCES

A **telling sentence** tells about something or someone. It begins with a capital letter. It ends with a **period** (.).

This frog sits in the pond.

Write these telling sentences correctly.

1. a frog can go

2. it has legs

3. it will jump

GRAMMAR

Teacher/Family Member: Children write telling sentences.

Name _____

ASKING SENTENCES

An **asking sentence** asks about something or someone. It begins with a capital letter. It ends with a **question mark** (**?**).

What will she see?

Two of these sentences are asking sentences.
Write the asking sentences correctly.

1. will you go with them

2. he jumps and plays

3. can she see the boat

Name _____

NAMING PARTS OF SENTENCES

A sentence has a **naming part.** It tells who or what the sentence is about.

The girls play.

Write the naming part of each sentence.

1. The friends play a lot. _____

2. A cat jumps up. _____

3. The duck is brown. _____

4. The dog jumps. _____

Teacher/Family Member: Children identify and write naming parts of sentences.

Name _____

JOINING NAMING PARTS

A sentence has a naming part. Sometimes the naming parts of two sentences can be joined.

Turtle looked.

Fox looked.

Turtle and Fox looked.

Join the naming parts of the sentences. Use the word and. Write the new sentences.

1. Turtle hid. Fox hid.

   _____
   _____
   _____

2. Cat played with Duck. Frog played with Duck.

   _____
   _____
   _____
   _____

GRAMMAR

Teacher/Family Member: Children write sentences and join naming parts.

Name _____

TELLING PARTS OF SENTENCES

A sentence has a **telling part.** It tells what someone or something does.

The game <u>starts</u>.

The friends <u>play</u>.

Write the telling part of each sentence.

1. The pig goes. _____

2. The fox plays. _____

3. They go. _____

4. Someone wins. _____

JOINING TELLING PARTS

A sentence has a telling part. Sometimes the telling parts of two sentences can be joined.

The birds fly. The birds sing.

The birds fly and sing.

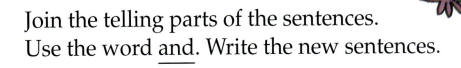

Join the telling parts of the sentences.
Use the word and. Write the new sentences.

1. The birds look. The birds flap.

2. The ducks quack. The ducks swim.

Name _____

IS IT A SENTENCE?

A **sentence** tells a complete thought. It has a naming part and a telling part. It begins with a capital letter. It may end with a **period (.)** or a **question mark (?)**.

They went walking.   Can you run?

Some of these groups of words are sentences. Write the sentences correctly.

1. in the sand

2. we have sand houses

3. is the sand wet

Name _____

WRITING I

The word I is always written as a capital letter.

Look how I can go!

Write each sentence correctly.

1. My friend and i play.

2. She and i have bikes.

3. you and i go fast.

4. Then i stop.

Name _____

END MARKS

A telling sentence ends with a **period** (.).

An asking sentence ends with a **question mark** (?).

The children have a chain.

Is the chain big?

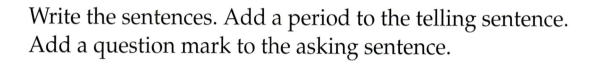

Write the sentences. Add a period to the telling sentence. Add a question mark to the asking sentence.

1. Can we fix the chain

2. This chain is big

Kids on Language

Teaching Spanish

My name is Evette. I speak English at school and Spanish and English at home. I think I could teach Spanish to people who speak only English. I would tell them the Spanish words for things like television set (televisor) or dog (perro). Or I might teach them to say "¡Hola!" ("Hello!") so that they could talk to Spanish people.

Teacher/Family Member: Read the paragraph aloud to children. Talk with them about their language.

NAMING WORDS

Naming words name people, places, or things.

Write the word that names people.

_____

1. My friends came with me. _____

Write the word that names a place.

_____

2. We walked to the park. _____

Write the word that names a thing.

_____

3. We went on the slide. _____

Name _____

NAMING WORDS FOR PEOPLE

Some naming words name **people.**

boy   doctor   teacher

Write the word that names a person in each sentence.

1. The girl lifts the basket.

2. My dad walks the dog.

3. The baby has little teeth.

4. The vet has a sick duck.

27

GRAMMAR

Teacher/Family Member: Children identify and write naming words for people.

Name _____

NAMING WORDS FOR PLACES

Some naming words name **places.**

school   city   woods

Write the word in each sentence that names a place.

1. Our friends are at school.
   _____
   _____

2. Baby birds walk on the beach.
   _____
   _____

3. I have four pups at my house.
   _____
   _____

4. Are there baby ducks in the park?
   _____
   _____

GRAMMAR

Teacher/Family Member: Children identify and write naming words for places.

Name _____

NAMING WORDS FOR ANIMALS AND THINGS

Some naming words name **animals** or **things**.

Write a word that names an animal or a thing. Use the picture.

1. Tanya has a _____.

2. She drinks from a _____.

3. It sits in a _____.

4. Look at my blue _____.

29
GRAMMAR

Teacher/Family Member: Children identify and write naming words for animals and things.

Name _____

SPECIAL NAMES AND TITLES OF PEOPLE

The **special name** of a person begins with a capital letter.

Tanya Wills

The **special title** of a person begins with a capital letter.

Dr. Fell

Write each special name or title correctly.

1. This basket is for sam.

2. His friend mr. Sanchez makes them.

3. Here are two baskets for sally.

Name _____

NAMES OF SPECIAL PLACES

The name of a **special place** begins with a capital letter.

We go to Clark School.

It is on Ash Street.

The school is in Glenbrook.

Write each name of a special place correctly.

1. My friend goes to west school.
   _____
   _ _ _ _ _ _ _ _ _ _ _ _ _ _ _ _
   _____

2. My school is on cheese road.
   _____
   _ _ _ _ _ _ _ _ _ _ _ _ _ _ _ _
   _____

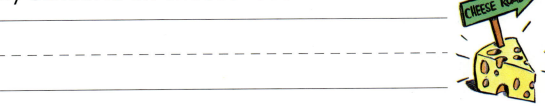

3. The schools are in redbird.
   _____
   _ _ _ _ _ _ _ _ _ _ _ _ _ _ _ _
   _____

Name _____

ONE AND MORE THAN ONE

A naming word can name **one**.

   finger

A naming word can name **more than one**. Some naming words add <u>s</u> to name more than one.

   finger<u>s</u>

Write the naming word that tells about the picture.

1. Where is one _____?
   bird   birds

2. Where are two _____?
   duck   ducks

3. Where are three _____?
   cat   cats

4. Where is one _____?
   dog   dogs

32

GRAMMAR

Teacher/Family Member: Children identify and write naming words that name one and more than one.

Name _____

DAYS OF THE WEEK

Some naming words name the **days of the week**. The names of the days of the week begin with capital letters.

Finish the sentences.
Write the names of the days of the week.

1. Today is _____.

2. Tomorrow is _____.

3. My favorite day of the week is _____.

Name _____

MONTHS

Some naming words name the **months of the year.** The names of the months begin with capital letters.

Write the name of a month to complete each sentence.

1. My birthday is in _____.

2. My favorite month is _____.

Name _____

HOLIDAYS

Some naming words name **holidays.** These words begin with capital letters.

Today is February 14.

It is Valentine's Day.

Write the name of each holiday correctly.

1. I get cards on valentine's day.

2. Let's plant a tree on arbor day.

3. Dad likes independence day.

4. Did you go away on thanksgiving day?

Name _____

USING I AND ME

The words **I** and **me** take the place of some naming words. Use **I** in the naming part of a sentence. Use **me** in the telling part of a sentence.

I am happy.

Grandma helps me.

Write I or me to complete each sentence.

1. _____ went to play.

2. Grandma saw _____.

3. She took _____ to lunch.

4. _____ love Grandma!

Name _____

USING HE, SHE, AND IT

The words **he**, **she**, and **it** take the place of some naming words.
Use **he** for a man or a boy.
Use **she** for a woman or a girl.
Use **it** for an animal or a thing.

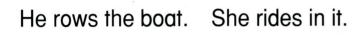

He rows the boat.   She rides in it.

Write he, she, or it to complete each sentence.

1. Today _____ helps her.

2. Then _____ gets a fish.

3. Oh, _____ is a big one!

Family Stories

People in my family love to tell stories. Sometimes the stories are just for kids. But sometimes they are for everyone to hear. At Kwanzaa, we take turns telling stories about our family. Everyone listens because the storyteller is talking about our family.

Name _____

DESCRIBING WORDS

Describing words tell about naming words.

The <u>brown</u> bear looks.

She catches a <u>little</u> fish.

Write the describing word in each sentence.

1. A black bear comes to the water.

2. Her little bear does, too.

3. They walk into the clean water.

4. The mother helps her wet cub.

39

GRAMMAR

Teacher/Family Member: Children identify and write describing words.

Name _____

FEELINGS

Some describing words tell how people **feel.**

Now Freddy is <u>sad</u>.

Freddy is <u>happy</u>.

Write each describing word that tells how Freddy feels.

1. When Freddy is tired, he goes to bed.

2. When Freddy is hungry, he eats.

3. When Freddy is hot, he looks for a fan.

4. When Freddy sees his friend, he is glad!

Name _____

SIZE AND SHAPE

Some describing words tell about **size** and **shape**.

big

small

round

square

Answer each question. Write the describing word that tells about size or shape.

1. What size is the basket?   big   brown

   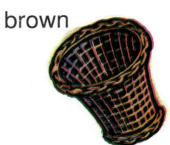

2. What size is a mouse?   red   small

3. What shape are apples?   round   square

Name _____

TASTE AND SMELL

Some describing words tell how things **taste** and **smell**.

This is <u>salty</u> popcorn.

The bread smells <u>fresh</u>.

Write each word that describes how something tastes.

1. My horse smells the sweet apples.
   _____
   _____

2. I taste the yummy berries.
   _____
   _____

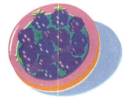

3. Dad finds a sour lemon.
   _____
   _____

4. Our dog tastes the salty water.
   _____
   _____

Name _____

COLORS AND NUMBERS

Some describing words tell **how many**. Some tell what **color**.

one two three

yellow green brown

Complete each sentence with a color or a number. Use the pictures to help you.

1. Three cookies are on a _____ plate.

2. I have _____ glass of pink lemonade.

3. Mom put _____ apples in a green basket.

4. Please give me ten _____ grapes.

43
GRAMMAR

Teacher/Family Member: Children identify and write describing words for color and number.

Name _____

FEEL AND SOUND

Some describing words tell how things feel. Some tell how things sound.

<u>soft</u> bed   <u>loud</u> clock

Read each sentence. Write the word that describes how something feels or sounds.

1. I like _____ chairs.
   soft   red

2. I like to read in _____ rooms.
   quiet   two

3. I like to walk in _____ grass.
   wet   green

4. I like to play in _____ places.
   long   noisy

Name _____

DESCRIBING WORDS WITH ER AND EST

Some describing words tell how things are different. Add **er** to tell how two things are different.

Some describing words tell how more than two things are different. Add **est** to tell how more than two things are different.

tall taller tallest

Write small, smaller, or smallest to complete each sentence.

1. The bed with stars is _____.

2. The bed with stripes is _____ than the one with stars.

3. The bed with dots is the _____ one of all.

GRAMMAR

Teacher/Family Member: Children identify and write describing words with er and est.

Name _____

DESCRIBING WORDS FOR WEATHER

Some describing words tell about the **weather.**

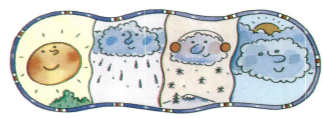

sunny   rainy   snowy   cloudy

Use one of the describing words to complete each sentence.

1. We can not see the sun on a _____ day.

2. What do deer do in _____ weather?

3. It is _____, so the foxes are playing.

4. The lions get wet when it is _____.

46

GRAMMAR

Teacher/Family Member: Children identify and write describing words for weather.

Kids on Language

Spanish and English Words

My name is Cesar. I speak two languages, English and Spanish. I like knowing how to say the same thing in two different ways. Sometimes I have to think fast to remember who I'm talking to! My grandmother lives in Lima, Peru. I call her "Ma Mama." When she comes to visit us, I speak only Spanish with her. When we go someplace or watch TV at my house, I help her with the English words.

Teacher/Family Member: Read the paragraph aloud to children. Talk with them about their language.

Name _____

ACTION WORDS

An **action word** tells what someone or something does.

 fly   plays   talks sleeps

Write the action word that completes each sentence.

1. Elena _____ with her doll.

2. The birds _____.

3. Her cat _____.

4. Mother _____ on the phone.

48 GRAMMAR

Teacher/Family Member: Children identify and write action words.

Name _____

ACTION WORDS ABOUT THE PAST

An action word can tell about the **past.** Some action words that tell about the past end with **ed.**

A mother duck <u>walked</u> across the grass.

She <u>quacked</u> for the little ducks.

Write the action words that tell about the past.

1. Two little ducks played in the water.

2. The mother duck looked at them.

3. Two little ducks jumped out of the water.

4. They all walked away.

49

GRAMMAR

Teacher/Family Member: Children identify and write past-tense action words ending in <u>ed</u>.

Name _____

ACTION WORDS ABOUT NOW

An action word can tell about **now**.

The raindrops <u>fall</u>.

The flowers <u>grow</u>.

Write the action words that tell about now.

1. The birds flap their wings.
   _____
   -
   _____

2. The children visit their friends.
   _____
   -
   _____

3. The boys play in the grass.
   _____
   -
   _____

4. The girls walk in water.
   _____
   -
   _____

50
GRAMMAR

Teacher/Family Member: Children identify and write present-tense action words.

Harcourt Brace School Publishers

Name _____

IS AND ARE

The words **is** and **are** tell about now.
Use **is** to tell about one person, place, or thing.
Use **are** to tell about more than one person, place, or thing.

One hen is asleep.

Two hens are awake.

Write is or are to complete each sentence.

1. Henny Penny _____ a hen.

2. Cocky Locky and Ducky Lucky _____
 _____ her friends.

3. Foxy Loxy _____ not her friend.

GRAMMAR

Teacher/Family Member: Children identify and write correct verb forms.

Name _____

GO AND WENT

The word **go** tells about now.
The word **went** tells about the past.

Jason went outside.

We go outside, too.

Write go or went to complete the story.

1. Yesterday I _____ to get a cat at the pet store.

2. Last night my cat _____ outside.

3. Now I _____ outside.

4. My cat and I _____ inside.

Teacher/Family Member: Children identify and write correct verb forms.

Name _____

WAS AND WERE

The words **was** and **were** tell about the past.
Use **was** to tell about one person, place, or thing. Use **were** to tell about more than one person, place, or thing.

One bear was lost.

The boy and the bear were not happy.

Write was or were to complete each sentence.

1. A boy and a bear _____ friends.

2. The bear _____ under the bed.

3. The boy _____ sad.

4. The friends _____ together again.

Chinese Alphabet

I went to visit my grandmother in Singapore. My mother and I rode in a jet for a very long time. My grandmother speaks only Chinese, so it was hard to talk to her. My mother taught me to say "Ma Ma Ping Ang." This means "Peace to Grandma" in Chinese. In Chinese writing, you would write it like this:

"媽媽平安"

Handwriting

Uppercase Manuscript Alphabet

ABCDEFGH
IJKLMNOP
QRSTUVW
XYZ

ABCDEFGH
IJKLMNOP
QRSTUVW
XYZ

Lowercase Manuscript Alphabet

Elements of Handwriting

Be sure that letters you write are not too close together or too far apart.

correct

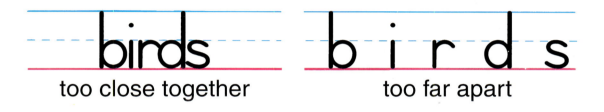
too close together   too far apart

Write the words.

1. bear   2. cat

3. duck   4. nest

Elements of Handwriting

Be sure the spacing between words is correct.

incorrect spacing

correct spacing

Write the sentences.

1. Today is sunny.

2. Summer is fun.

3. You can swim.

Common Errors — Manuscript Letters

Write the letters correctly.

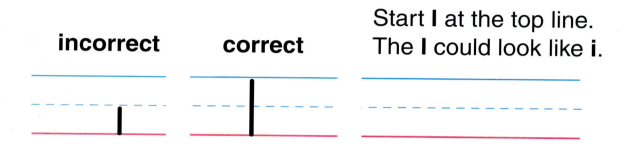

Start **l** at the top line.
The **l** could look like **i**.

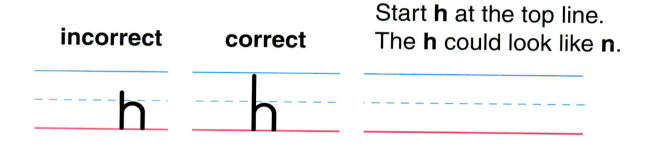

Start **h** at the top line.
The **h** could look like **n**.

incorrect   **correct**

Touch the bottom line.
The **n** could look like **r**.

Common Errors — Manuscript Letters

Write the letters correctly.

incorrect **correct** Do not close **c**.
The **c** could look like **o**.

incorrect **correct** Curve to the left.
The **d** could look like **b**.

incorrect **correct** Close **o**.
The **o** could look like **c**.

Common Errors — Manuscript Letters

Write the letters correctly.

incorrect	correct	
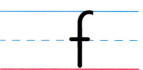		Circle left. The **f** could look like **t**.

incorrect	correct	
		Close **a**. The **a** could look like **u**.

incorrect	correct	
		Start the second stroke at the midline. The **k** could look like uppercase **K**.

incorrect	correct	
		Start **x** at the midline. The **x** could look like uppercase **X**.

Common Errors — Manuscript Letters

Write the letters correctly.

incorrect **correct** Cross **T** at the top line.
The **T** could look like **I**.

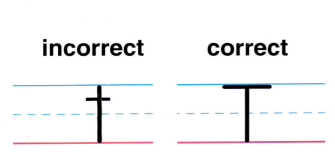

incorrect **correct** Use all the touchpoints.
The **E** could look like **F**.

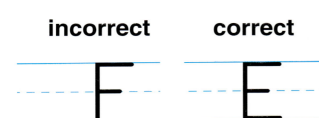

incorrect **correct** Use the short slant stroke.
The **Q** could look like **O**.

Common Errors — Manuscript Letters

Write the letters correctly.

incorrect **correct**

C G

Use the straight across stroke.
The **G** could look like **C**.

incorrect **correct**

O U

Make your strokes go straight up and down.
The **U** could look like **O**.

incorrect **correct**

B R

Do not curve the slant stroke.
The **R** could look like **B**.

HANDWRITING

Harcourt Brace School Publishers

Common Errors — Manuscript Letters

Write the letters correctly.

incorrect **correct**

Curve to the bottom line.
The **D** could look like **P**.

incorrect **correct**

Stop at the bottom line.
The **M** could look like **N**.

incorrect **correct**

Go to the bottom line two times.
The **W** could look like **V**.

incorrect **correct**

Start at the top line.
The **Z** could look like lowercase **z**.

HANDWRITING

Name _____

SENTENCES ABOUT A PICTURE
Teacher/Family Member: Children can use this page when they draw a picture and write sentences about it. (See page 3.)

Name _____

STORY

Teacher/Family Member: Children can use this page when they write a story. (See pages 4 and 8.)

Name _____

Teacher/Family Member: Children can use this page when they write a poem. (See page 5.)

Name _____

FRIENDLY LETTER

Teacher/Family Member: Children can use this page when they write a friendly letter. (See page 6.)

Name _____

Title

Author

What is this book about?

What is your favorite part?

BOOK REPORT

Teacher/Family Member: Children can use this page when they write a book report. (See page 10.)

Action words, 48
    about now, 50
    about the past, 49
Are, 51
Asking sentence, 17

Book report, 10

Capital letters
    days, 33
    holidays, 35
    I, 23
    months, 34
    sentences, 14, 16, 17, 22
    special names of people, 30
    special places, 31
    titles of people, 30
Captions, 3
Common errors—manuscript letters, 60–65
Composition, 2–12

Days of the week, 33
Describing words, 39
    colors, 43
    feel, 44
    feelings, 40
    number, 43
    size, 41
    shape, 41
    smell, 42
    sound, 44
    taste, 42
    weather, 46
    with *er* and *est*, 45
Description, 7

Elements of handwriting, 58–59
End marks, 24
    period, 16, 22, 24
    question mark, 17, 22, 24
er, *est*, 45

Friendly letter, 6

Go, 52
Grammar, 14–54

Handwriting, 56–65
He, 37
Holidays, 35
How-to sentences, 11

I, 23, 36
Information sentences, 3
Is, 51
It, 37

Joining naming parts, 19
Joining telling parts, 21

Kids on Language, 25, 38, 47, 54

Letter
    See Friendly letter.
Letters of the alphabet, 56–57
Lowercase manuscript alphabet, 57

Me, 36
Months of the year, 34

Naming parts of a sentence, 18, 19
Naming words, 26
    animals, 29
    people, 26, 27
    places, 28, 31
    one and more than one, 32
    special names of people, 30
    things, 29
    titles of people, 30

Period
    usage, 24
    identifying, 22
    telling sentences, 16
Poem, 5
Punctuation
    end marks, 16, 17, 22, 24
    in a friendly letter, 6
    of titles of people, 30

Question mark
    asking sentence, 17
    definition, 24
    identifying, 22

Riddle, 9

Scene, 12
Sentences, 14
    about a picture, 3
    asking, 17
    how-to, 11
    identifying, 22
    joining naming parts, 19
    joining telling parts, 21
    naming parts, 18
    telling, 16
    telling parts, 20
    word order, 15
She, 37
Story, 8
    about you, 4

Telling parts of a sentence, 20, 21
Telling sentences, 16
Titles of people, 30

Uppercase manuscript alphabet, 56
Usage
    go and *went*, 52
    he, she, and *it*, 37
    I and *me*, 36
    was and *were*, 53

Was, 53
Went, 52
Were, 53
Word order in sentences, 15
Writing forms
    book report, 10
    description, 7
    friendly letter, 6
    how-to sentences, 11
    poem, 5
    riddle, 9
    scene, 12
    sentences about a picture, 3
    story, 8
    story about you, 4
Writing process, 2